Seriously WTF is Wrong with Men

Seriously WTF is Wrong with Men

Jordan Reid

Illustrations by Kelly Lasserre

A TARCHERPERIGEE BOOK

tarcher perigee

an imprint of Penguin Random House LLC
penguinrandomhouse.com

Copyright © 2020 by Jordan Reid

Illustrations by Kelly Lasserre

TarcherPerigee with tp colophon is a registered trademark of Penguin Random House LLC

Most TarcherPerigee books are available at special quantity discounts for bulk purchase for sales promotions, premiums, fund-raising, and educational needs. Special books or book excerpts also can be created to fit specific needs. For details, write: SpecialMarkets@penguinrandomhouse.com.

ISBN 9780593085936

Printed in the United States of America
1 3 5 7 9 10 8 6 4 2

To all the boys I've loved before:
This one's for you.

WHAT. THE ACTUAL. FUCK.

— all women, everywhere

Hi!
Before we get started,
let's do a disclaimer!
FUN. STUFF.

This highly scientific, 100% fact-based exploration of male psychology was based entirely on highly scientific, 100% fact-based conversations with my friends.

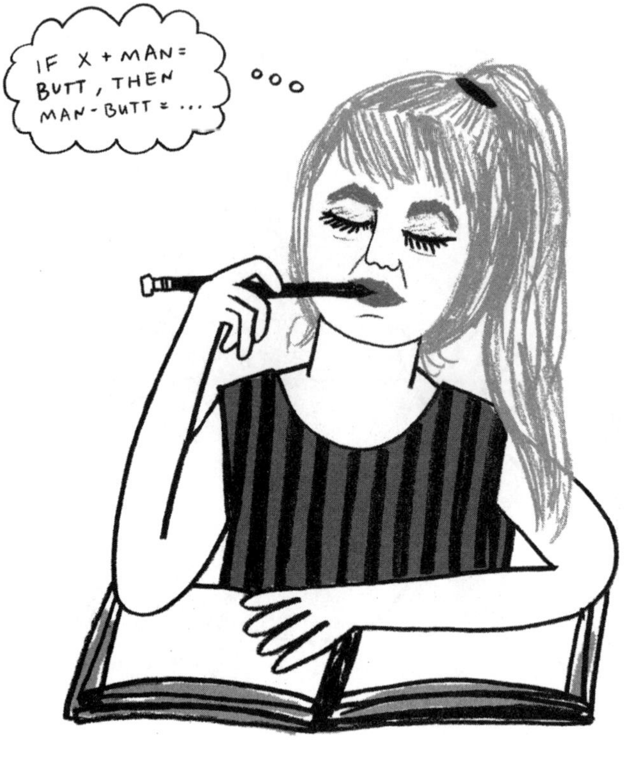
IF X + MAN = BUTT, THEN MAN-BUTT = ...

None of whom "hate men."
Some of them even report
loving one! OR MANY!
Imagine!

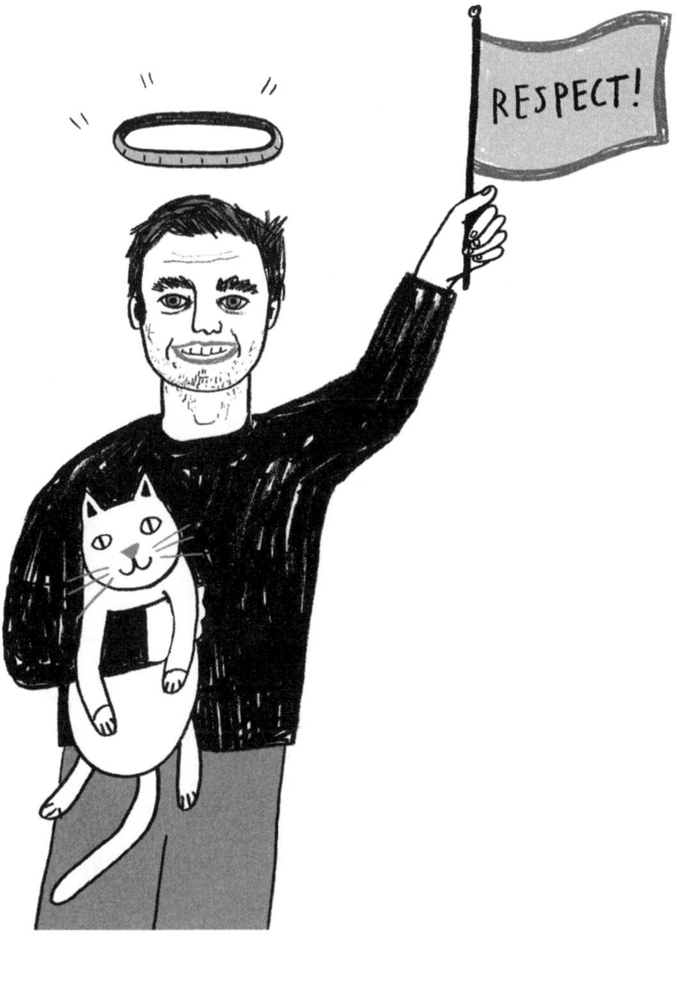
RESPECT!

And of course,
in every population
there are outliers.

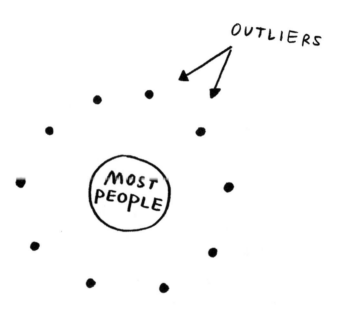

OUTLIERS

MOST PEOPLE

OUTLIER:
out·li·er / out līər/
thing that allegedly exists once in a while
(see also: flying pigs)

You may even personally know a few of these shining beacons of humanity!

YOUR DAD
MOST PEOPLE
YOUR BROTHER
YOUR POSTMATES DELIVERY GUY

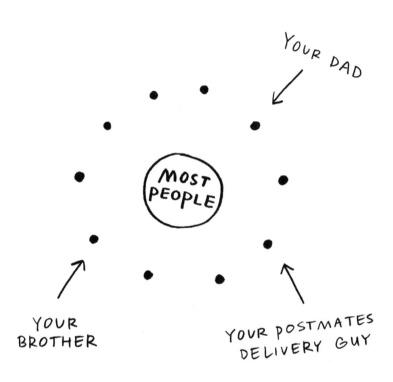

So.
Some men are great.
maybe even *most* men!

But it's still a fact that not a single fucking one of them can successfully put a dirty sock into a hamper.

FACT:

/fakt/

a thing that is known or proved to be true. because I said so.

Now that we're on the
same page ...

Shall we begin ?

WTF-ery at Home

If there is a God,
I am convinced
he is a he,
because no
woman
could or would
fuck things up
this badly.

— GEORGE CARLIN

MEN & LAUNDRY BASKETS:
an analysis (in two parts)

PART ONE: WHY?

BEAUTIFUL,
DISCREETLY
PLACED
LAUNDRY BASKET

DIRTY SOCKS
NEXT TO LAUNDRY
BASKET ON FLOOR

PART TWO: **BECAUSE.**

TILTING BASKET
45° ANGLE
FOR APPROPRIATE
SOCK PLACEMENT
WAY TOO HARD

ERGO SOCKS
MUST GO HERE

THESE ARE NOT EXAMPLES OF "HELPING"

CARING FOR CHILDREN TO WHOM YOU CONTRIBUTED GENETIC MATERIAL

BUYING FOOD THAT NO ONE BUT YOU WANTS TO EAT

CHEEZY
YUCK
YUCK
GROSS
BAD

WASHING CLOTHING THAT
YOU YOURSELF MADE SMELL
LIKE A GERIATRIC CAMEL

FIXING THINGS THAT
NEED TO BE FIXED
IN THE HOUSE
THAT YOU LIVE IN

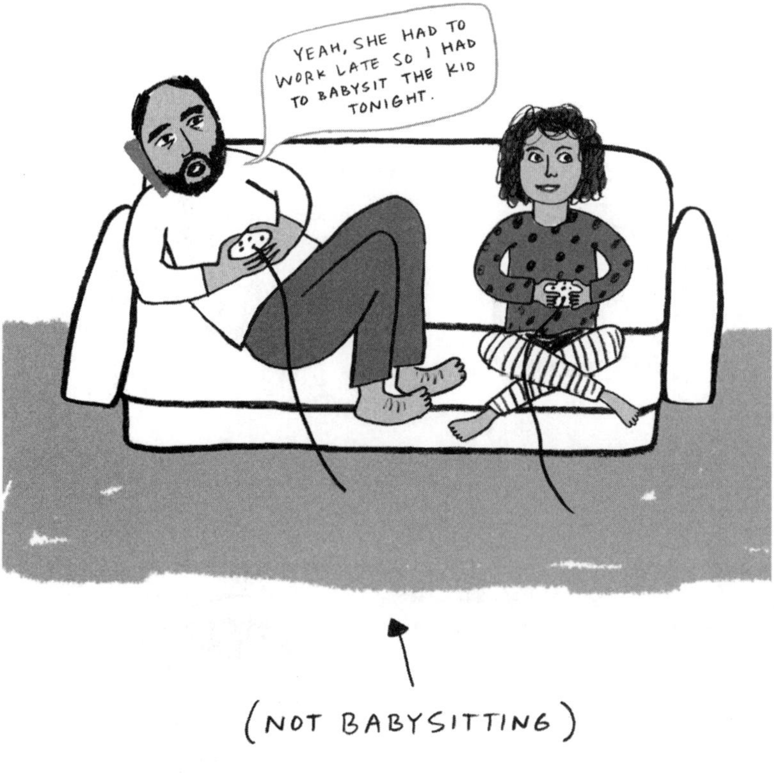
YEAH, SHE HAD TO WORK LATE SO I HAD TO BABYSIT THE KID TONIGHT.
(NOT BABYSITTING)

Me: CAN YOU RUN TO THE GROCERY STORE REAL QUICK? WE NEED SOME MILK.

Three and a half hours later...

He: (RETURNS WITH THINGS AND STUFF.)
(FEELS TRIUMPHANT.)

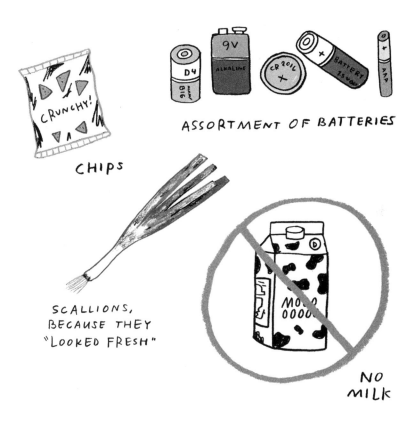

CRUNCHY!

CHIPS

D4
9V
ALKALINE
CR 2016
BATTERY
AAA

ASSORTMENT OF BATTERIES

SCALLIONS, BECAUSE THEY "LOOKED FRESH"

NO MILK

Scene:

WE OPEN ON THE MOTHER,
BUSTLING ABOUT IN THE LIVING ROOM.

SHE HAS JUST SPENT THREE STRAIGHT
DAYS PREPARING FOR HER 6-YEAR-OLD'S
BIRTHDAY PARTY.

SHE HAS HANDCRAFTED 8 VISUALLY APPEALING GAMES, ASSEMBLED 25 PARTY-FAVOR BAGS (WITH ORGANIC TREATS!), PINTEREST-SOURCED RECIPES FOR CARROT FRIES WITH LEMON-AIOLI DIP, SEMOLINA AND SUNDRIED TOMATO WAFFLE SQUARES AND BAKED MACARONI AND CHEESE CUPCAKES.

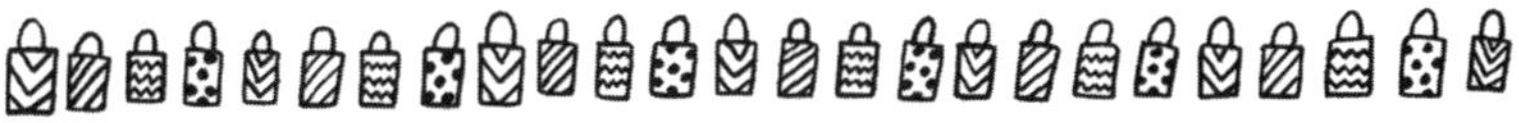

SHE HAS LEARNED HOW TO FONDANT, AND HAS USED SAID NEWLY ACQUIRED KNOWLEDGE TO FONDANT A CAKE IN THE SHAPE OF THE MAIN CHARACTER FROM THE TELEVISION SHOW *PINKALICIOUS*.

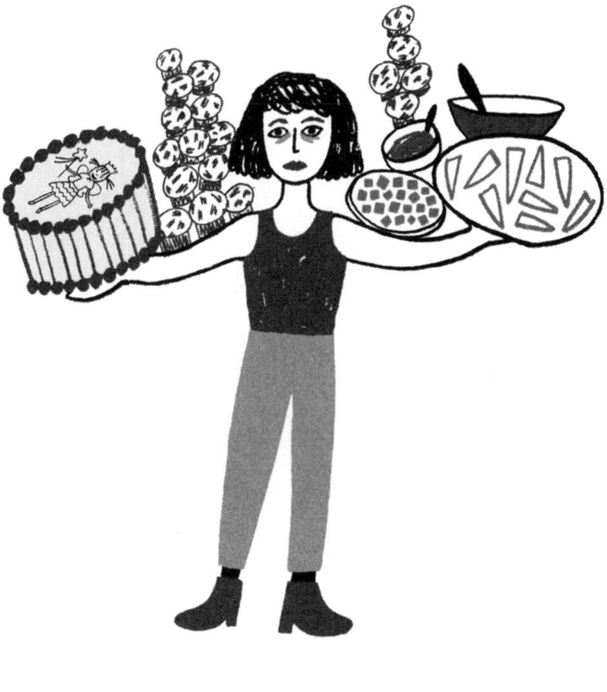

The Father enters the room.

FATHER: "Wow! Looks amazing!
Can I help with anything?"

MOTHER: "Actually... Yeah.
Can you order the pizza?"

FATHER: "Of course! Anything else
you need, just say the word!"

It is two hours later.

GAMES HAVE BEEN PLAYED,
SEMOLINA HAS BEEN CONSUMED,
AND EVERYONE IS READY FOR PIZZA.

THE PIZZA IS NOT THERE.

MOTHER TO FATHER:

" You ordered the pizza, right? "

FATHER: (GENUINELY CONFUSED)

"You never gave me the phone number to the pizza place."

WTF-ERY THROUGHOUT HISTORY

Ronald Wayne, the third cofounder and 10% shareholder of Apple, decided to sell his stock. In 1976. For $800. Wooops.

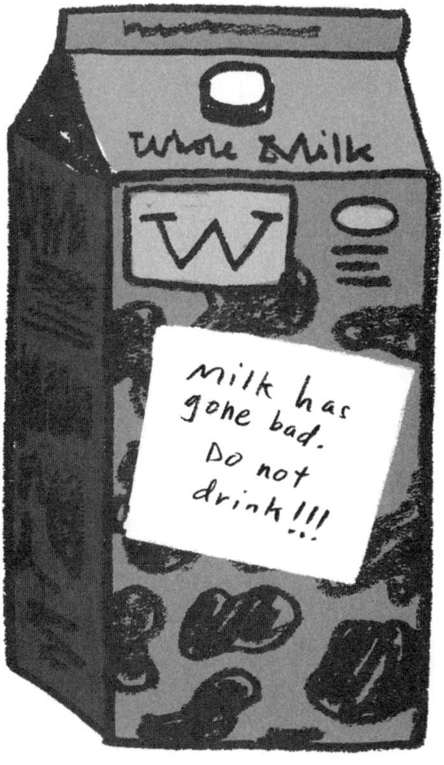
Whole Milk
W
milk has gone bad. Do not drink!!!

THIS SEEMS LIKE THE LOGICAL SOLUTION TO THE PROBLEM.

Rationalizations that are no bueno:

"What? I'm going to need to get
something out of them
again at some point."

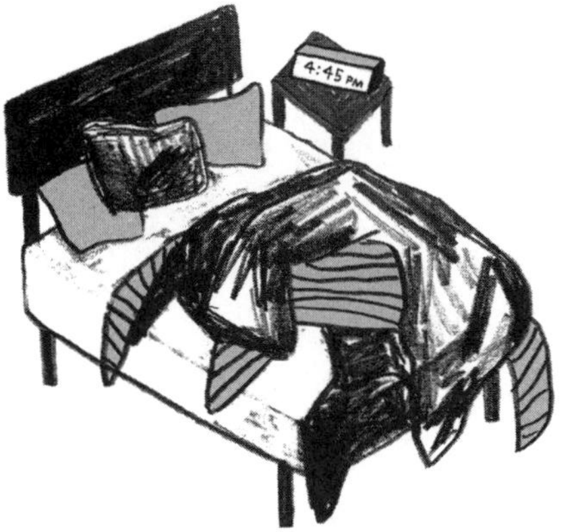
4:45 PM

"What? I'm going to sleep in it again at some point."

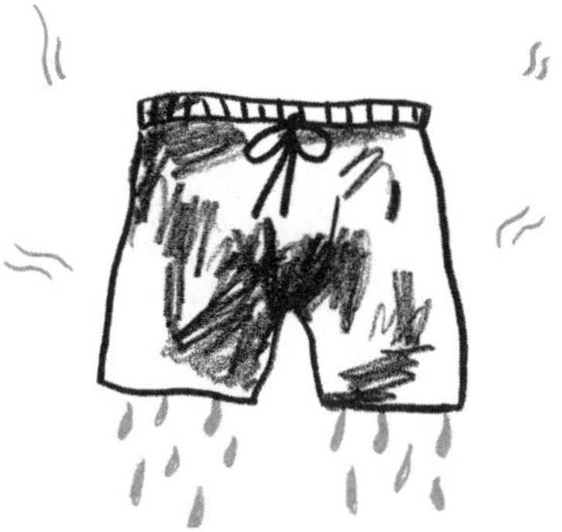

"What? I'm going to work out again at some point."

Things That Are Apparently Not Ready to Be Thrown Out

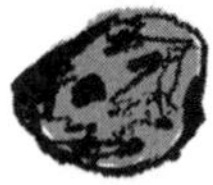

COOKIE BOX WITH 1/8TH
OF 1 COOKIE LEFT

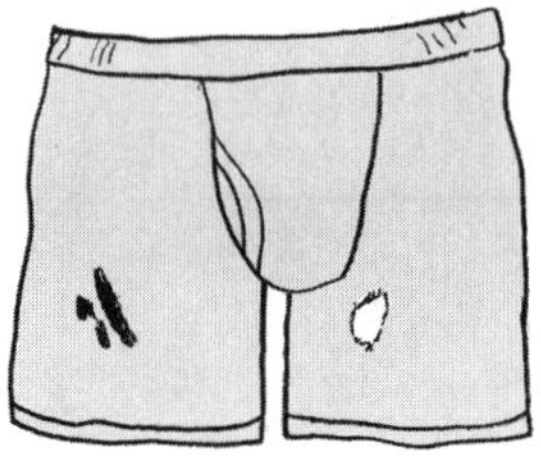

THIS PAIR OF
UNDERWEAR

THIS PAIR
OF SHOES

VHS OF FAVORITE
PORN FROM 1996

ANY SOCKS
AT ALL, EVER

HER:

COULD YOU GRAB AIDEN'S BATMAN BACKPACK?
IT'S ON THE KITCHEN COUNTER, RIGHT IN BETWEEN
THE SINK AND THE COFFEE MAKER.

HIM:
(returns from kitchen)
SORRY, COULDN'T FIND IT.

TEXT MESSAGES FROM FRIENDS

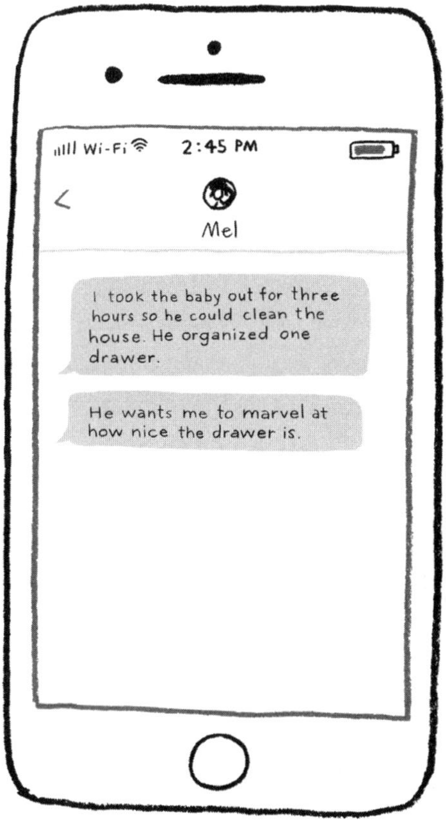

Wi-Fi
2:45 PM
Mel
I took the baby out for three hours so he could clean the house. He organized one drawer.
He wants me to marvel at how nice the drawer is.

[REDACTED] AND I HAVE A CALIFORNIA KING-SIZE BED, WHICH IS HUGE. HE SLEEPS ON THE SIDE NEAREST THE BEDROOM DOOR, ABOUT TEN FEET FROM THE ENTRANCE TO THE KITCHEN. EVERY NIGHT OF HIS LIFE, HE MUST HAVE A GLASS OF WATER BY HIS BED. OF COURSE, HE NEVER DRINKS IT, BUT HE DOESN'T WANT TO DRINK "OLD WATER," SO THEN THE NEXT NIGHT HE GOES AND GETS A NEW GLASS OF WATER. HE BRINGS THE NEW WATER BACK TO OUR BEDROOM, PUTS IT ON HIS NIGHTSTAND, AND WALKS THE OLD WATER ALLLLLLL THE WAY AROUND OUR BED SO THAT HE CAN PUT IT DOWN. ON MY NIGHTSTAND.

WHY.

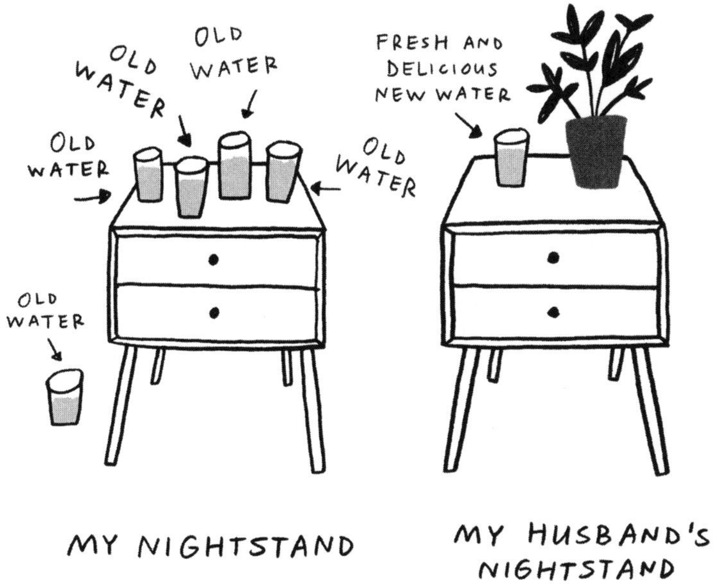
OLD WATER
OLD WATER
OLD WATER
OLD WATER
OLD WATER
FRESH AND DELICIOUS NEW WATER
MY NIGHTSTAND
MY HUSBAND'S NIGHTSTAND

THESE THINGS DO NOT GO ON THE MANTEL

DEAD
BATTERY
COLLECTION

ELECTRIC
RAZOR

CANS OF
FRESCA

PLASTIC
ACTION
FIGURES

DOG
HAIR

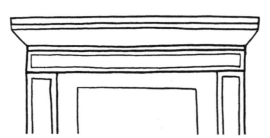

A NEW PURCHASE FOR THE BATHROOM!

WHAT SHE SEES

ELEGANT, QUALITY FIXTURES →

A GREAT PRICE, THANKS TO HOURS OF RESEARCH

GORGEOUS CRAFTSMANSHIP →

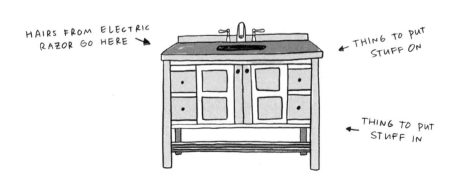

WHAT HE SEES

HAIRS FROM ELECTRIC RAZOR GO HERE →

← THING TO PUT STUFF ON

← THING TO PUT STUFF IN

Things a Man Cannot Do When Afflicted with the Sniffles:

Work

Move

Handle any basic household responsibilities whatsoever

Feed self

Stop moaning

(Thumbs still
work though!)

RESPONSIBILITY IS EXHAUSTING

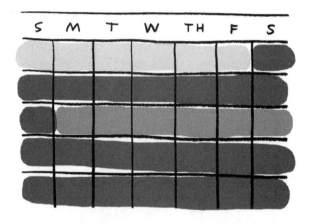

	S	M	T	W	TH	F	S

☐ HUSBAND AWAY ON A BUSINESS TRIP

◻ WIFE AWAY ON A BUSINESS TRIP

◼ HUSBAND NEEDS "A BREAK"

Attention to detail is hard

I FELT LIKE CRAP LAST NIGHT SO [REDACTED] SAID HE'D
PUT THE BABY TO BED.

LATER THAT NIGHT I WENT IN TO
KISS OUR SLEEPING NINE-MONTH-OLD GOOD NIGHT.

HE PUT THE BABY TO BED!

NAKED.

WTF-ERY THROUGHOUT HISTORY

A GROUP OF NASA ENGINEERS TOOK BEING NOT-SUPER-DETAIL-ORIENTED TO THE NEXT LEVEL WHEN THEY USED THE ENGLISH SYSTEM OF MEASUREMENT TO NAVIGATE A VESSEL ORBITING MARS, WHILE THE REST OF THE TEAM USED THE METRIC SYSTEM.

THIS RESULTED IN THE ORBITER LITERALLY GETTING LOST IN SPACE, TO THE TUNE OF $125 MILLION DOLLARS.

THIS IS NOT FOR YOU.

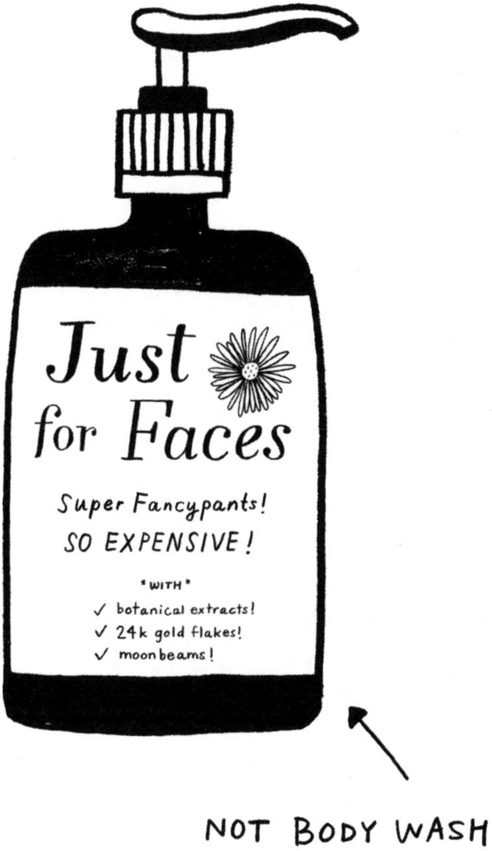
Just for Faces
Super Fancypants!
SO EXPENSIVE!
WITH
✓ botanical extracts!
✓ 24k gold flakes!
✓ moonbeams!
NOT BODY WASH

VACATION PREP

Her To-Do List

PACK FOR SELF
PACK FOR KIDS
PACK FOR EMERGENCIES
PACK CHARGERS
PACK TOILETRIES
DOWNLOAD BOOKS
DOWNLOAD EMERGENCY CONTACTS
DOWNLOAD DESTINATION INFORMATION
THROW OUT PERISHABLES
CLEAN REFRIGERATOR
RUN DISHWASHER
MAKE BED
CONFIRM HOTEL RESERVATION
CONFIRM FLIGHT RESERVATION
CONFIRM CAR RESERVATION
CONFIRM PET SITTER
CHECK ALARM
CHECK WINDOWS
CHECK MAIL
CHECK TO-DO LIST
WORRY

VACATION PREP

His To-Do List

PACK FOR SELF
SIT VERY, VERY STILL
ASK WHY IT TAKES SO LONG TO GET OUT OF THE HOUSE

Your Child's Lunch

FANCY BENTO BOX THING

↓

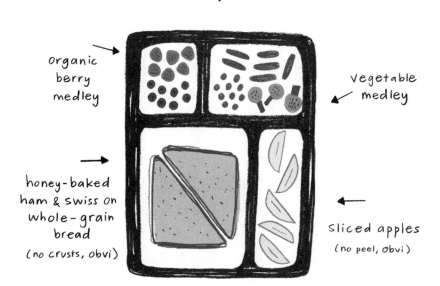

organic berry medley

vegetable medley

honey-baked ham & swiss on whole-grain bread
(no crusts, obvi)

Sliced apples
(no peel, obvi)

YOU MADE IT, PER USUAL.

FANCY BENTO BOX THING

fritos

rice

rice

rice

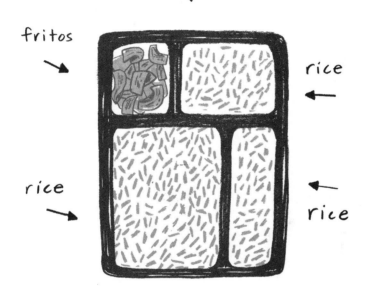

YOU MADE THE DIRE
MISTAKE OF OUTSOURCING.

Steps for Opening a Bottle

1. Remove bottle opener from drawer.

2. Open bottle.

3. Return bottle opener to drawer.

4. Put bottle cap in drawer, too.
   (Might come in handy later.)

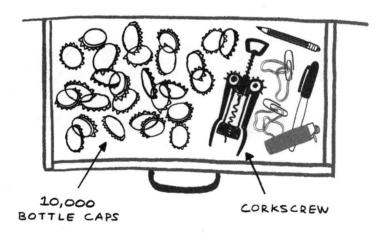

10,000
BOTTLE CAPS

CORKSCREW

THINGS REQUIRED TO HANG A PICTURE ON A WALL

- NAIL
- HAMMER
- TAPE MEASURE
- LEVEL
- 5 POSTPONEMENTS (MINIMUM)
- BEER (ASSORTED)
- EMOTIONAL SUPPORT
- SO MUCH GRATITUDE
- A NICE LONG REST

WTF-ERY THROUGHOUT HISTORY

In 2008, Father Adelir Antonio, a 42-year-old priest, attempted to pull off a PR stunt to support his goal of building a "spiritual rest stop" for truckers, which is nice. Unfortunately, his plan was to beat the 19-hour flight record held by Lawnchair Larry, who famously attached 45 balloons to his lawn chair and took off through the Los Angeles sky. Because Lawnchair Larry survived, Father Antonio figured he would, too.

He would not. Turns out that even though he did survival training and test flights, he neglected to figure out how to use the GPS tracking system that he brought with him—and so when the wind shifted and took him off-course, he disappeared forever.

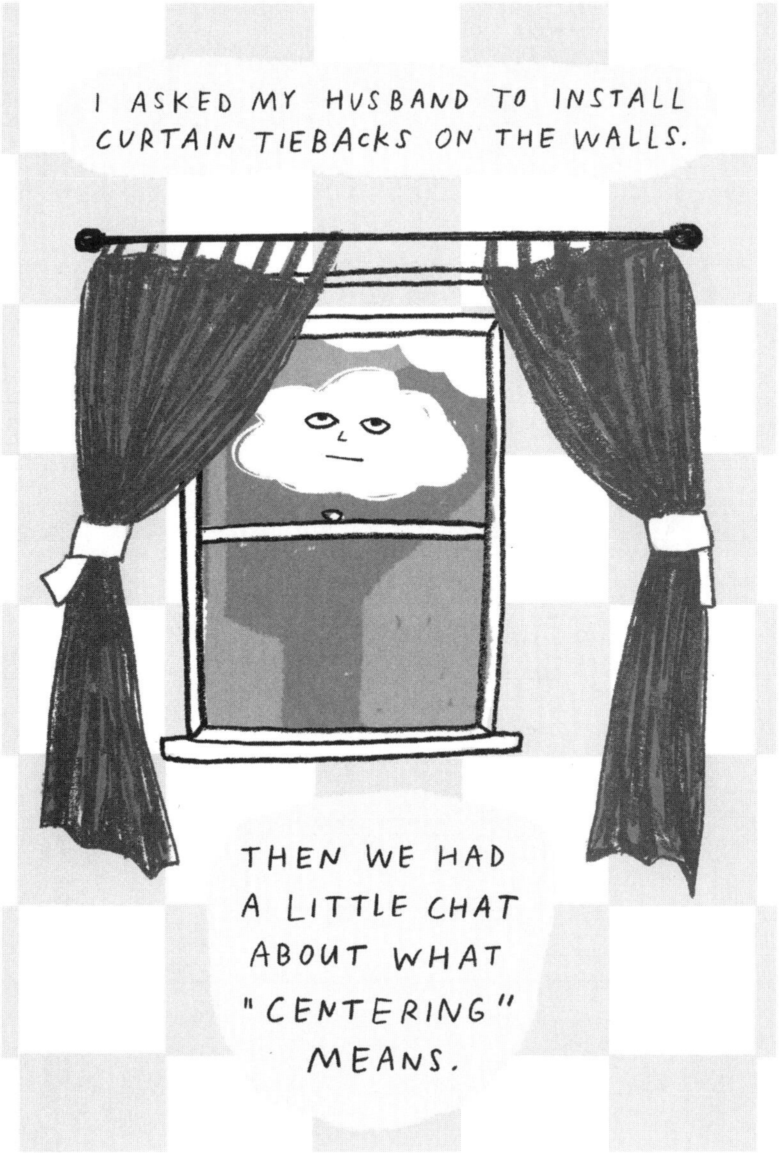
I ASKED MY HUSBAND TO INSTALL CURTAIN TIEBACKS ON THE WALLS.
THEN WE HAD A LITTLE CHAT ABOUT WHAT "CENTERING" MEANS.

Put Together IKEA Dresser,
Is Basically Superhero *

* NO SARCASM HERE, ANYONE WHO CAN PUT
TOGETHER AN IKEA DRESSER GETS A PRIZE.

In Praise of TaskRabbit

	YES	NO	POSSIBLY
Comes (and goes) on command	X		
Knows where the goddamn Allen wrench is	X		
Asks how your day is going	X		
Genuinely cares how your day is going			X
Will not interrupt your nap with question #643	X		
Can be paid in cash, as opposed to guilt	X		
Is cute			X
Is mostly silent			X
Will drink the last Diet Coke in the fridge and forget to tell you		X	

CAN YOU IMAGINE
A WORLD
WITHOUT MEN ?
THERE'D BE NO CRIME,
AND LOTS OF FAT,
HAPPY WOMEN.

— Nicole Hollander

ADD YOUR OWN
WTF-ery at Home:

WTF-ery in the Wild

A man is just
a woman's
strategy
for making
other
women.

— MARGARET ATWOOD

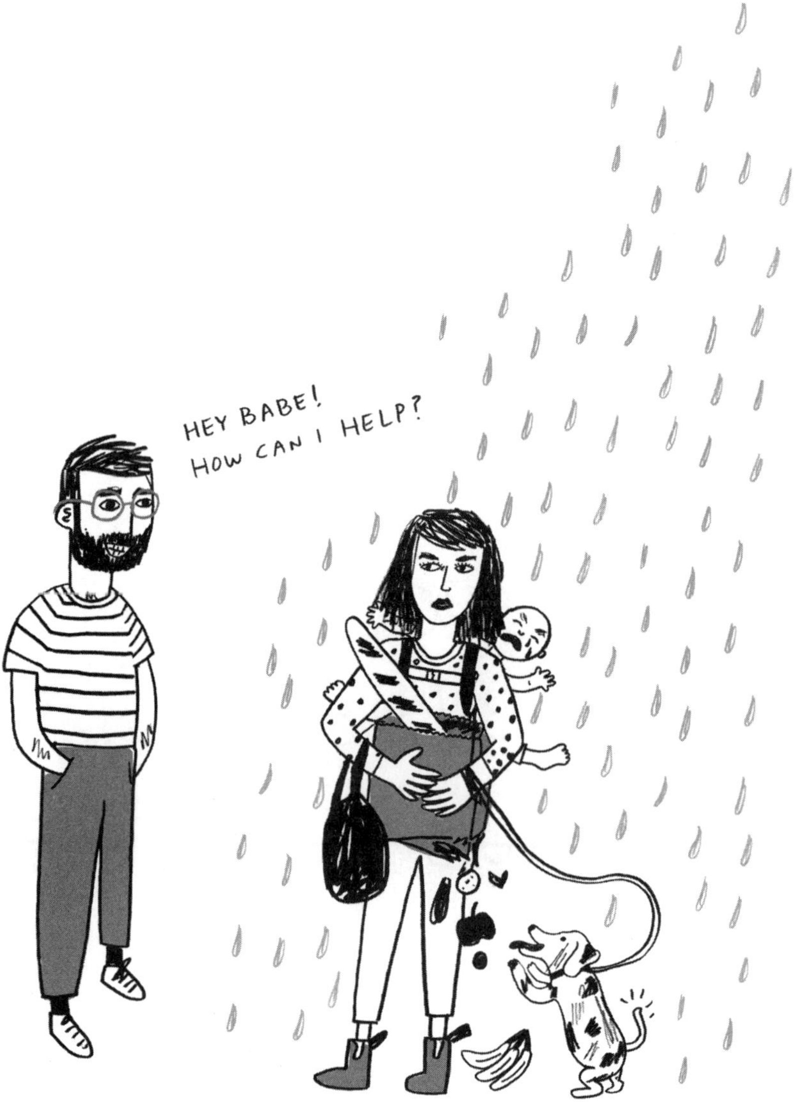
HEY BABE!
HOW CAN I HELP?

Fun Fact:

FOR APPROXIMATELY
THE FIRST SIX WEEKS
AFTER CONCEPTION,
ALL HUMAN EMBRYOS
DEVELOP AS A DEFAULT
FEMALE CHILD,
PRIMARILY TAKING GENETIC
INFORMATION FROM
THE MOTHER'S DNA.

IN OTHER WORDS,
ALL MEN STARTED OUT AS
WOMEN.

THINGS THAT YOU WILL NOT BE SURPRISED TO LEARN WERE INVENTED BY MEN:

- "BUTT-CHUGGING," the practice in which alcohol is ingested directly through... the butt.

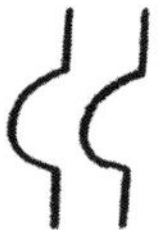

- FLESHLIGHTS, sex toys that look exactly how you think they look, and function exactly how you think they function.

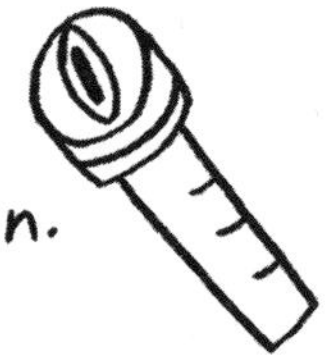

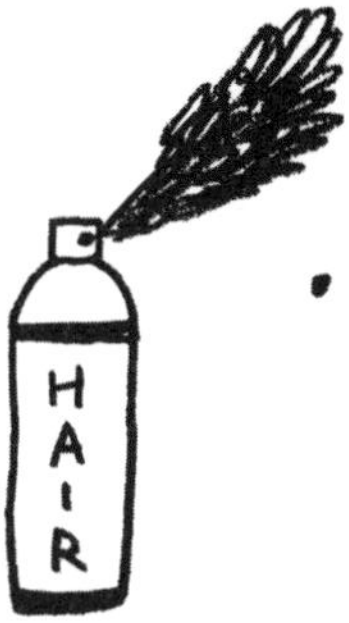
HAIR

- HAIR IN A CAN.
  Don't worry,
  NO ONE CAN TELL.

- BIKINIS,
  because of course.

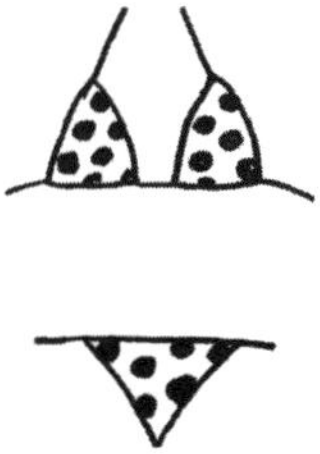

- TAMAGOTCHIS, tiny machines that one's children are theoretically responsible for keeping alive, but that will clearly not stay alive if left to children, making them one more fucking thing their mother has to deal with.

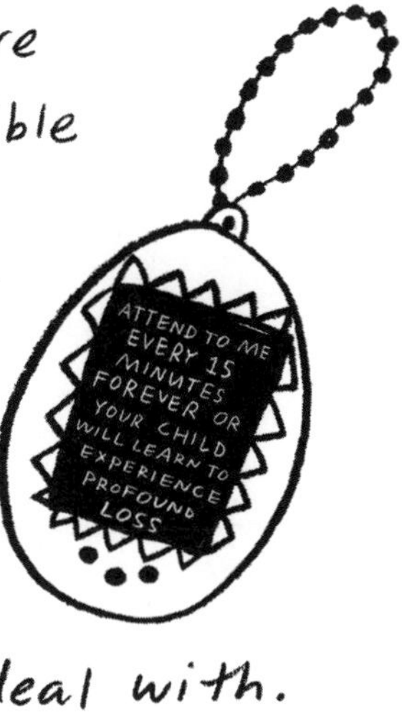
ATTEND TO ME EVERY 15 MINUTES FOREVER OR YOUR CHILD WILL LEARN TO EXPERIENCE PROFOUND LOSS

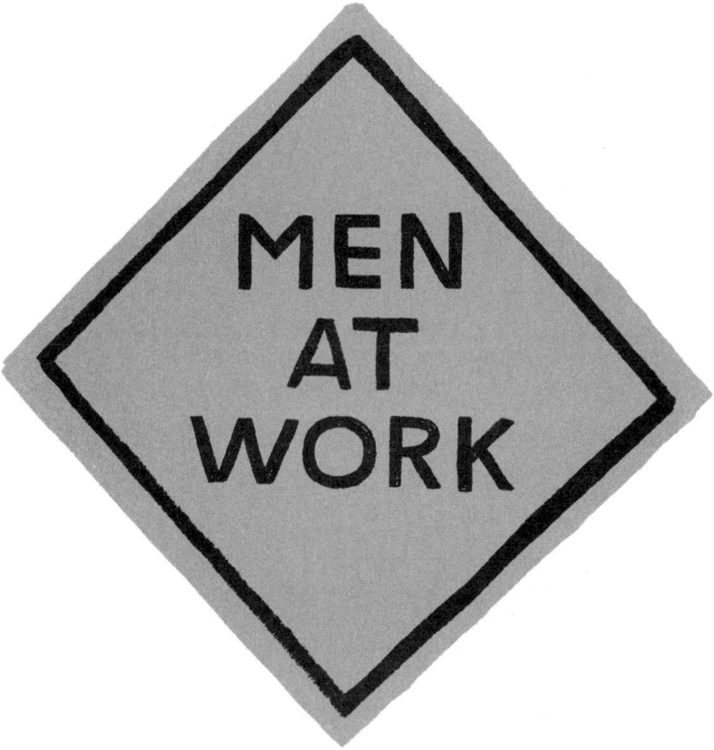
MEN
AT
WORK

Because when men are doing something,

EVERYONE MUST KNOW.

WTF-ERY THROUGHOUT HISTORY

In 1409, THREE POPES WERE ELECTED AT THE SAME TIME. AND OF COURSE THEY REACTED IN THE ONLY RATIONAL WAY: BY TRYING TO EXCOMMUNICATE EACH OTHER.

Things You Didn't Know Men Do and Now Can Never Un-Know*

** Mostly having to do with their penises, because most of these are sourced from Reddit. Sorry.*

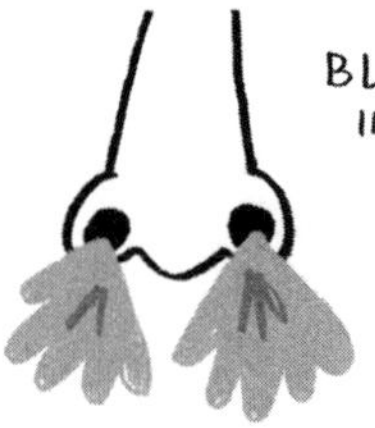

BLOW THEIR NOSES IN THE SHOWER

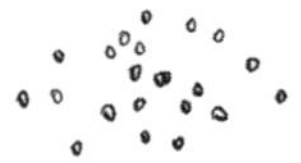

CHASE THEIR PEE BUBBLES AROUND THE BOWL WITH THEIR URINE STREAM

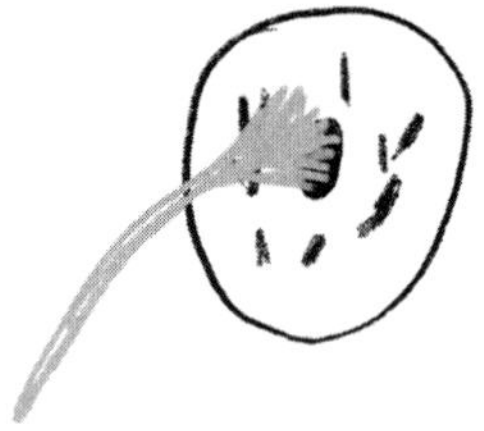

PEE ON THE POOP MARKS. YOU KNOW, TO CLEAN THEM.

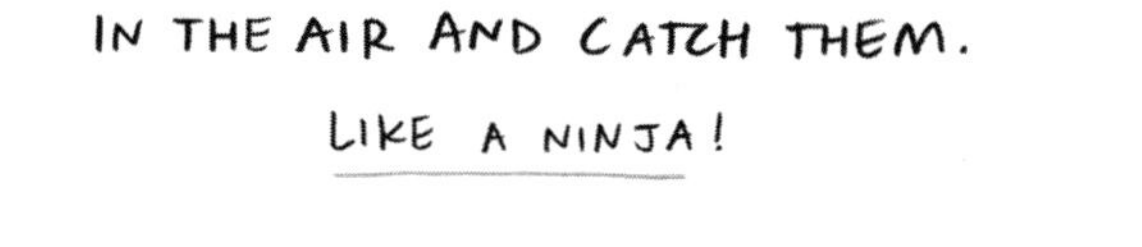

KICK THEIR DIRTY GYM SHORTS UP IN THE AIR AND CATCH THEM.

LIKE A NINJA!

SCRATCH THEIR BALLS
THROUGH THEIR POCKETS

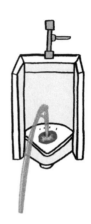

TRY TO BORE
HOLES THROUGH
URINAL CAKES
WITH THEIR
SHEER
MALE POWER

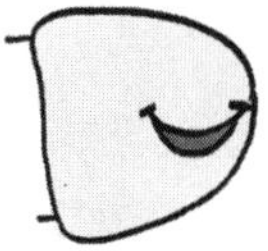

MAKE THE TIP OF THEIR
PENIS OPEN AND CLOSE LIKE
A TEENY-TINY MOUTH

SQUEEZE THEIR BUTTS
IN ORDER TO
MOVE THEIR PENISES

GET PEE ON THE WALL
EVEN THOUGH THEY'RE
OLDER THAN SIX

MAN-SPREADING:
A RATIONALIZATION

APPROXIMATE
DIAMETER OF
DEATH STAR

- AM NOT LADY → DESERVE MORE SEAT
(ALSO MORE MONEY, POWER AND CONTROL OVER OTHER PEOPLE'S REPRODUCTIVE DECISIONS)

- HAVE BIG VIRILE MANPARTS
→ CANNOT RISK CRUSHAGE

- LITTLE BUDDIES DON'T LIKE TO BE CONFINED
→ MUST LISTEN TO LITTLE BUDDIES

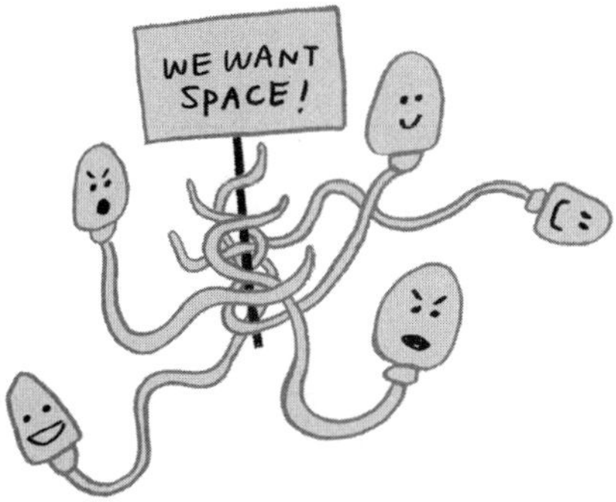
WE WANT SPACE!

- MY COMFORT >
YOUR DESIRE NOT TO LOOK AT MY INNER THIGHS

- AT LEAST AM NOT WEARING A KILT

HIS MOST FAVORITEST UNDERWEAR: A DIAGRAM

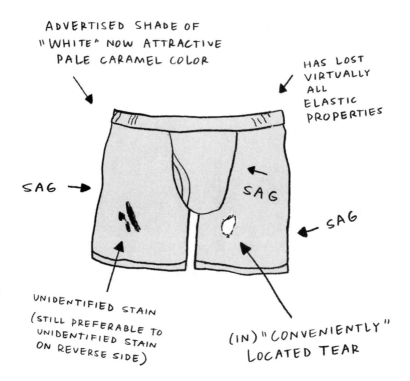

ADVERTISED SHADE OF "WHITE" NOW ATTRACTIVE PALE CARAMEL COLOR

HAS LOST VIRTUALLY ALL ELASTIC PROPERTIES

SAG →

SAG

SAG

UNIDENTIFIED STAIN (STILL PREFERABLE TO UNIDENTIFIED STAIN ON REVERSE SIDE)

(IN) "CONVENIENTLY" LOCATED TEAR

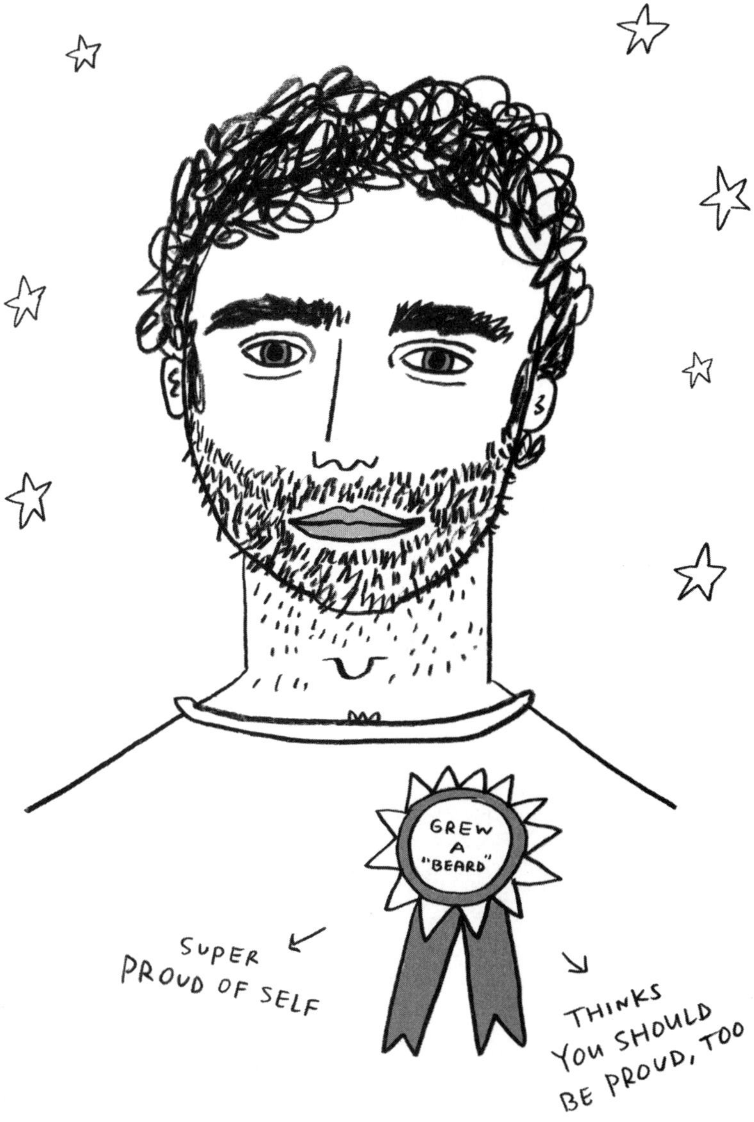
GREW A "BEARD"
SUPER PROUD OF SELF
THINKS YOU SHOULD BE PROUD, TOO

IN HOME DEPOT

Hi, I'm redoing our bathroom and was wondering what kind of tile grout would work best in a high-moisture area?

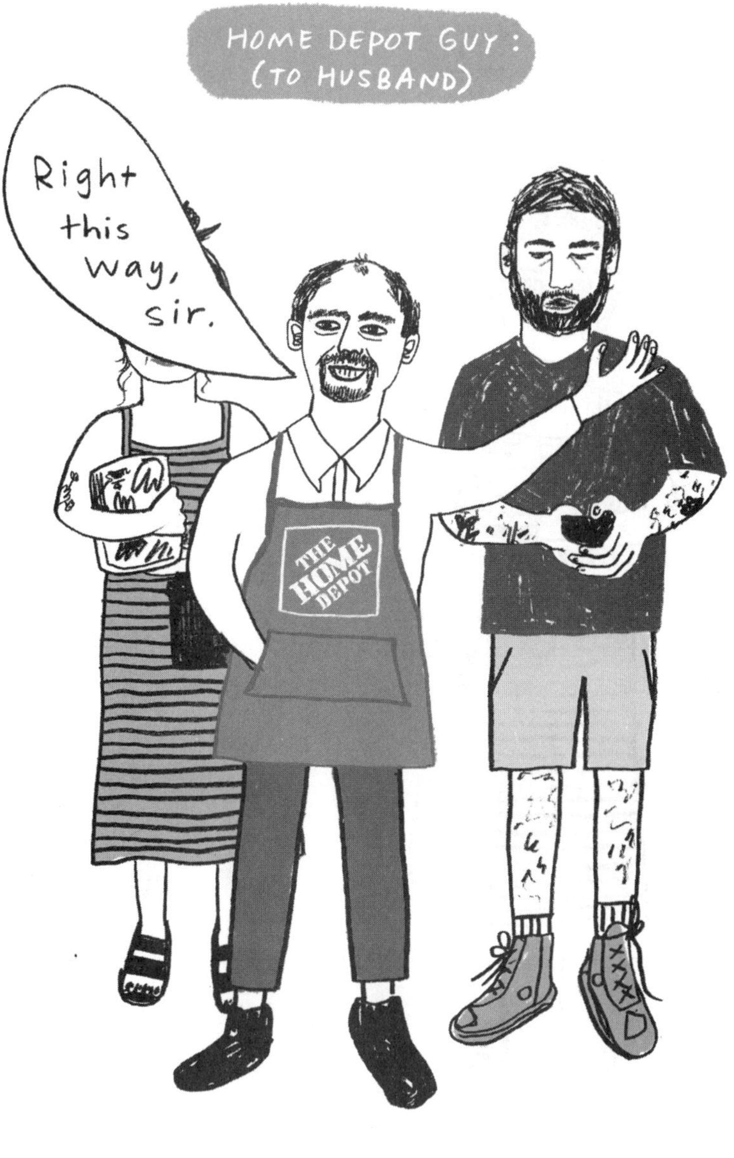
HOME DEPOT GUY: (TO HUSBAND)
Right this way, sir.
THE HOME DEPOT

PINTEREST FOR BOYS

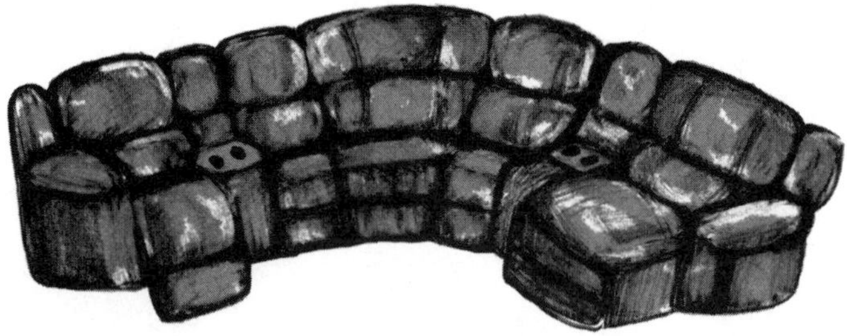

BLACK LEATHER SECTIONAL
WITH CUP HOLDERS & RECLINERS

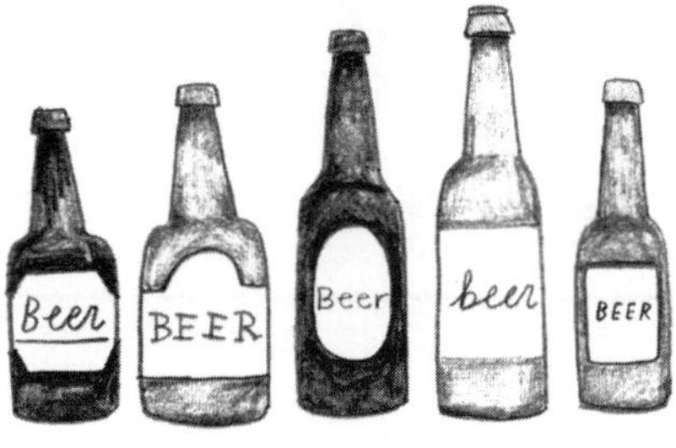
Beer
BEER
Beer
beer
BEER

BEER BOTTLE
"COLLECTION"

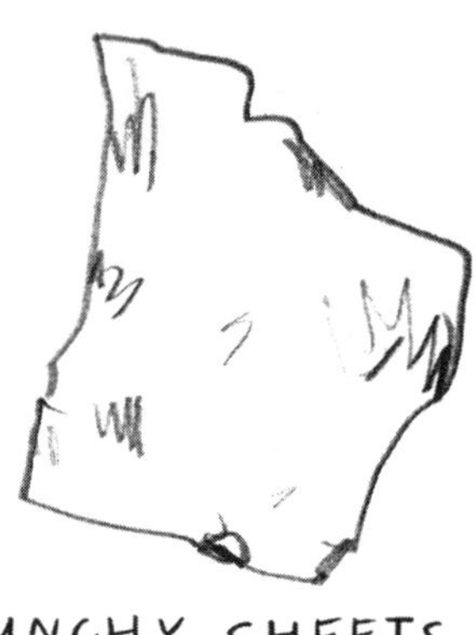

CRUNCHY SHEETS

AGGRESSIVE
GAMING STATION

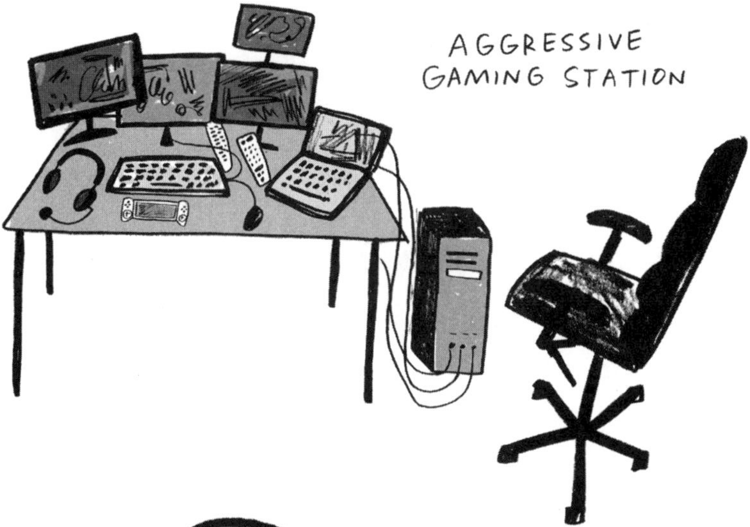

TUBA
TOILET

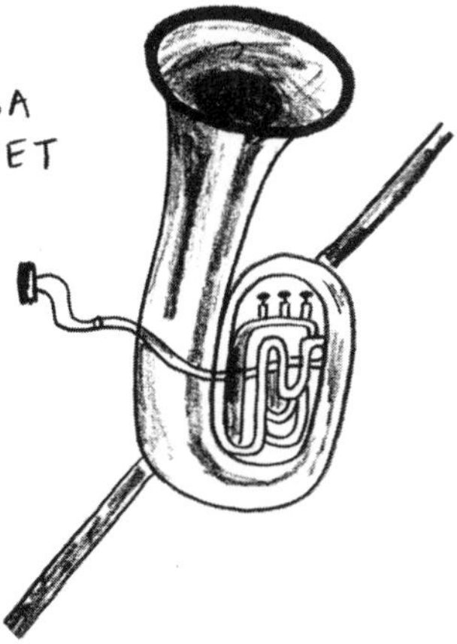

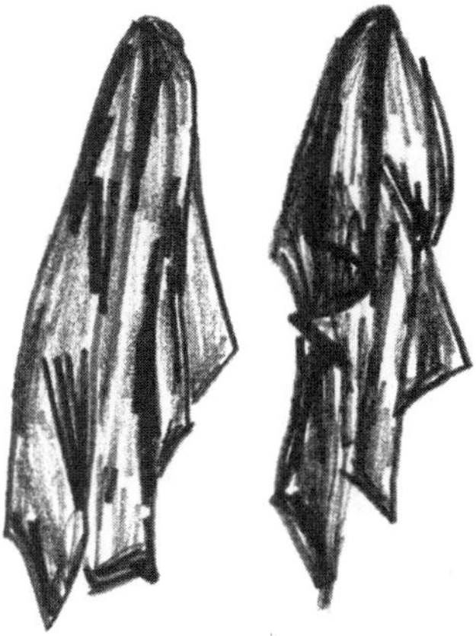

RED OR BLACK BATH TOWELS

IN THE WOMAN'S BRAIN

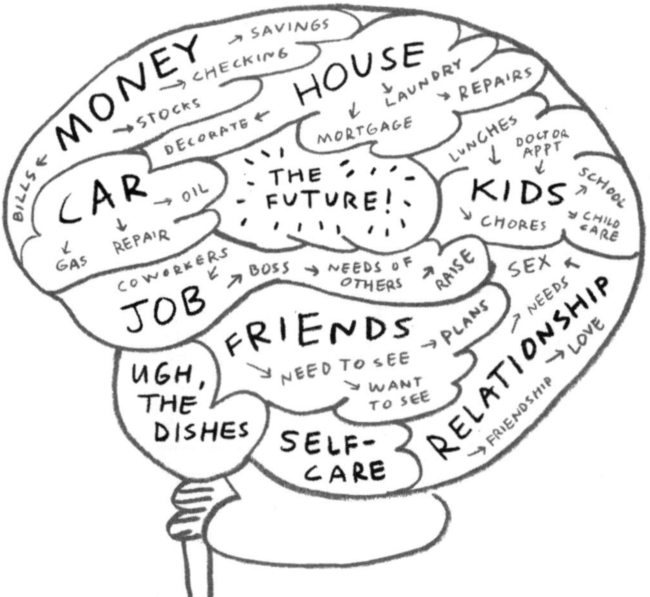
MONEY
SAVINGS
CHECKING
STOCKS
BILLS
HOUSE
LAUNDRY
REPAIRS
MORTGAGE
DECORATE
CAR
OIL
REPAIR
GAS
THE FUTURE!
KIDS
LUNCHES
DOCTOR APPT
SCHOOL
CHORES
CHILD CARE
JOB
COWORKERS
BOSS
NEEDS OF OTHERS
RAISE
SEX
FRIENDS
PLANS
NEED TO SEE
WANT TO SEE
RELATIONSHIP
NEEDS
LOVE
FRIENDSHIP
UGH, THE DISHES
SELF-CARE

IN THE MAN'S BRAIN

MAN VS. WILD
ME
ME, ME, ME
ME
ME
ME
CAN MY PENIS GO HERE?
ME
ME
ME
ME
ME
ME
ME
ME
ME
ME
ME
ME
ME
ME
ME ME ME
REDDIT
ME
ME
ME ME
ME
CHICKEN
BOOBS
ME
ME
ME
ME ME
ME

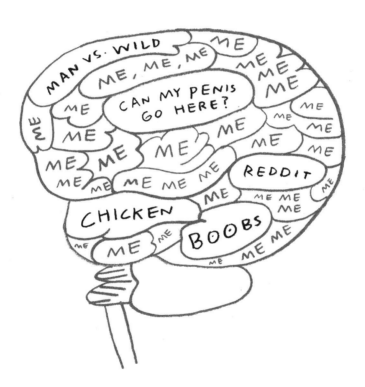

ABSOLUTELY DO NOT DATE THESE MEN

IG "INFLUENCER" MAN

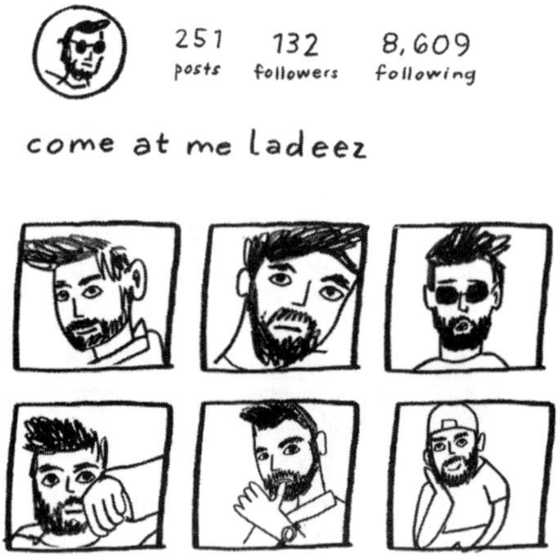
251 posts
132 followers
8,609 following
come at me ladeez

LOOSE EYEBALLS MAN

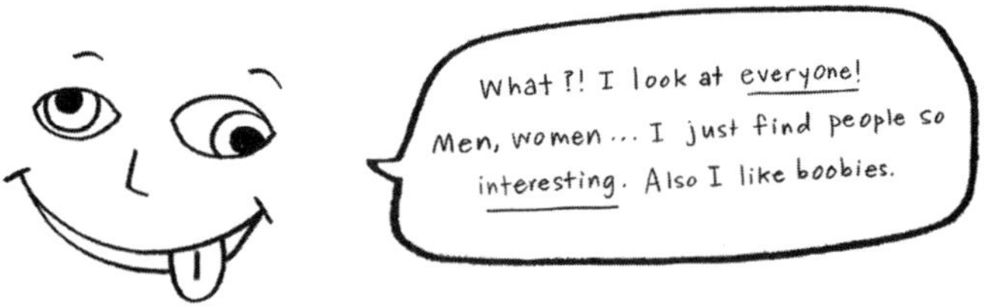
What?! I look at everyone! Men, women... I just find people so interesting. Also I like boobies.

LOVE BOMBER MAN

I love you more than anyone I've
ever loved EVER.* After just
two days! Isn't it CRAZY?!
Let's move in together!
Let's get married!
Let's get impregnating !!! **

* EXCEPT FOR LEONA, WHO I SAID THESE EXACT WORDS TO LAST
WEEK. BUT YOU'RE DIFFERENT. SO! SPECIAL! TRUST ME!

** ALSO, DO NOT DATE ANY MAN THAT USES THE WORD
"IMPREGNATE" IN ANY FORM, FOR ANY REASON WHATSOEVER.

BASKETBALL SHORTS MAN

We. Can see.
Your penis.
Always.

DATING OPTIONS, IN EDIBLE TERMS

HOSTESS CUPCAKE

* SUPER YUMMY. ZERO NUTRITIONAL VALUE.

Example:

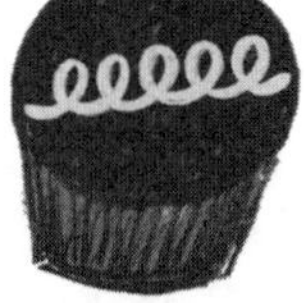

- DECADE-TOO-YOUNG "FILMMAKER"
- THINKS KISSING = FACE-EATING COMPETITION

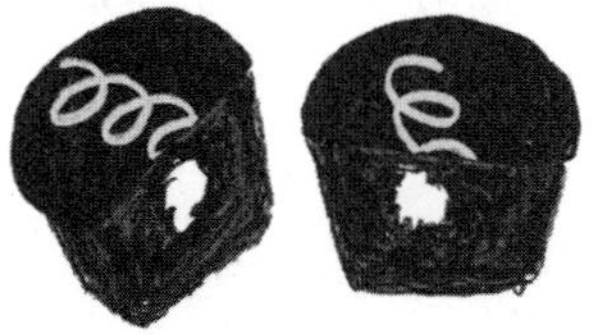

- WANTS TO TELL YOU ABOUT THE SCREENPLAY HE IS WORKING ON

ARTICHOKE

* EXCITING AND DESIRABLE, BUT A HUGE PAIN IN THE ASS TO GET TO THE HEART.

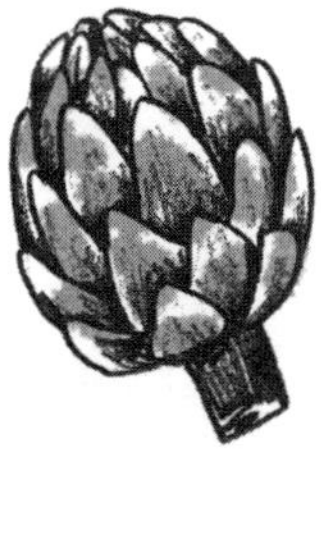

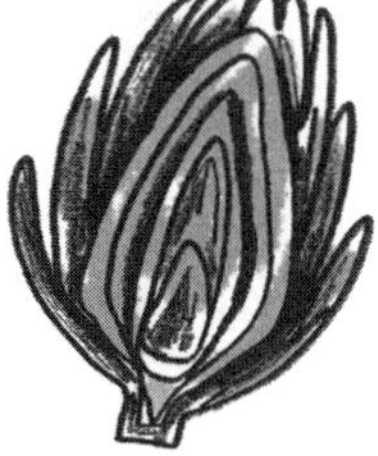

Example:

- ER DOCTOR MET VIA APP
- ALSO DATING 15 OTHER WOMEN MET VIA APP

COCONUT

* RARE AND ELUSIVE, MOSTLY EXPERIENCED IN SAD IMITATION FORM (EG: COCONUT WATER)

Example:

- AGE-APPROPRIATE, EMOTIONALLY EVOLVED HUMAN

- UNDERSTANDS BASIC CONCEPT OF FIDELITY

- HAS A JOB!

ROTTEN COCONUT

* MIGHT LOOK LIKE SOMETHING YOU CAN HANDLE FROM THE OUTSIDE, BUT SMOOSHY AND TERRIFYING ONCE YOU GET IN THERE.

Example:

- DECADE-TOO-OLD REPUBLICAN

- STILL LIVES WITH ESTRANGED WIFE

- BROKE UP WITH YOU BEFORE YOU COULD BREAK UP WITH HIM

THIS MAN DEFINITELY WANTS SOMEONE TO **POOP** ON HIM

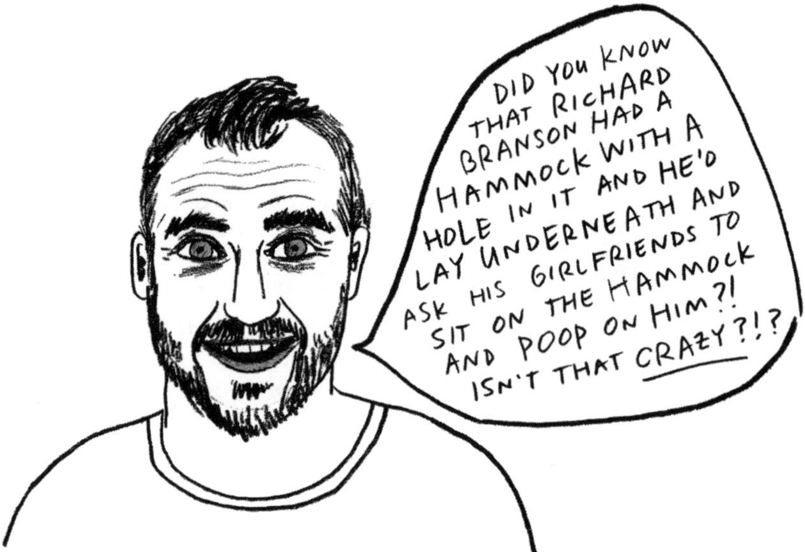
DID YOU KNOW THAT RICHARD BRANSON HAD A HAMMOCK WITH A HOLE IN IT AND HE'D LAY UNDERNEATH AND ASK HIS GIRLFRIENDS TO SIT ON THE HAMMOCK AND POOP ON HIM?! ISN'T THAT CRAZY?!?

WTF-ERY THROUGHOUT HISTORY

ATTILA THE HUN WAS SO IN LOVE WITH HIS BRIDE-TO-BE THAT HE FELT THE NEED TO DESTROY ITALY EN ROUTE TO PICKING HER UP.

Bathroom Texts with Friends

information acquired within 1st half hour of tonight's date:
he was in a cult for ten years; he had a horrible sex life with his wife; his wife recently left him for a festival DJ named ravensbreath lovepowder; he doesn't think he believes in monogamy.

bless.

the sum total of the information he has acquired about me :
1. my gender, and 2. my name (maybe).

and now he is watching the game while i sit next to him with my club soda

and he has a massive stye on his eye

help

YOUR FIRST FIVE INSTA-STORY VIEWS, LIKE EVERY TIME

BEST FRIEND

GUY WHO GHOSTED YOU

YOUR MARRIED EX

GUY WHO YOU TEXTED WITH 87,000 TIMES BUT NEVER ACTUALLY MET IRL

HI MOM

 HI.

Places we do not want to be hit on:

- On the elliptical
- On an airplane
- On the subway
- On our doorstep
- Costco

DATING APP CONVERSATIONS YOU DON'T WANT TO HAVE

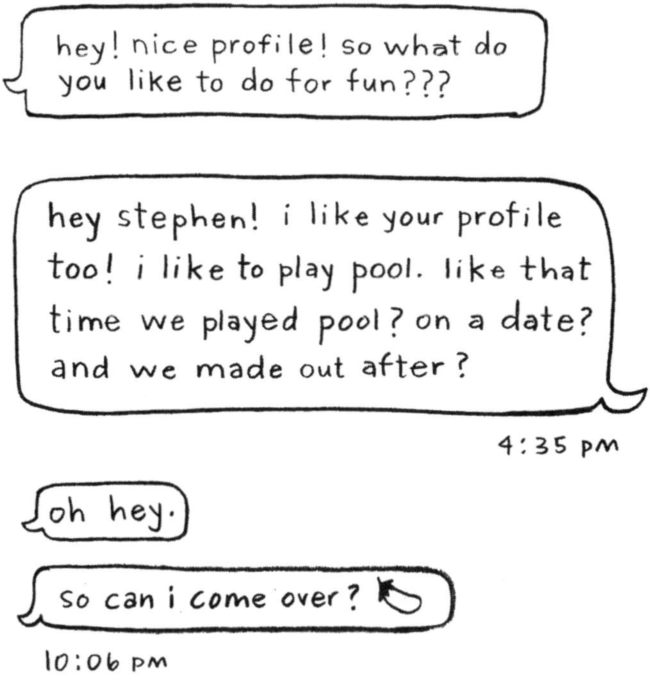
hey! nice profile! so what do you like to do for fun???
hey stephen! i like your profile too! i like to play pool. like that time we played pool? on a date? and we made out after?
4:35 pm
oh hey.
so can i come over?
10:06 pm

Completely Unacceptable Emojis to Receive from a Potential Date

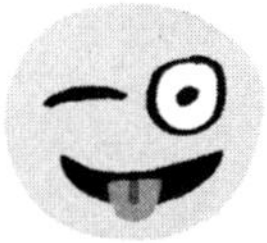

Imagine someone making this face at you IRL.

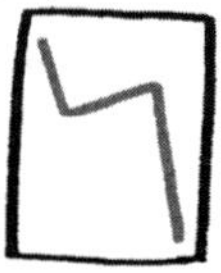

"Everything is fucked."
Hot.

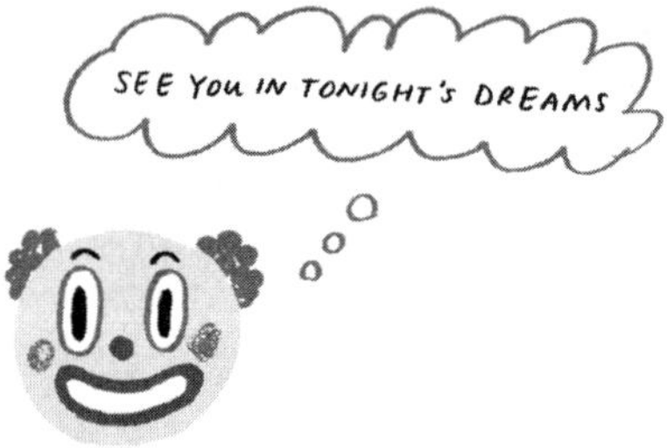
SEE YOU IN TONIGHT'S DREAMS

This emoji exists solely to communicate high levels of potential psychopath-ness. Run away. Quickly. Not upstairs though.

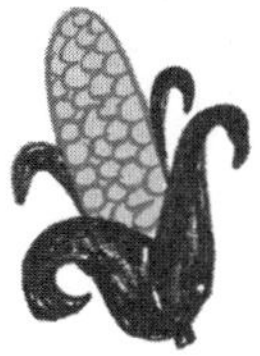

We see you trying to talk about your penis
without going full eggplant.
YOU DO NOT FOOL US.

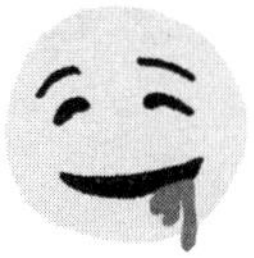

Are you... okay?
Do you require medication?

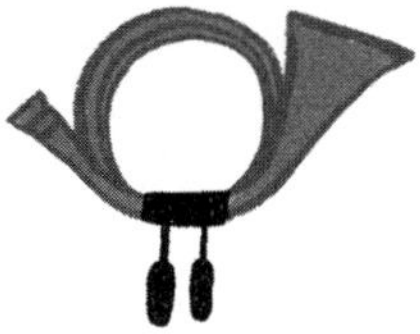

"You remind me of an obscure woodwind instrument that nobody would play if their parents hadn't made them so they'd get into college on the highly coveted 'postal horn' scholarship."

5 TYPES OF BAD KISSERS

The Tongue Darter

The Face Eater

The Dainty Pecker

The Cardio Enthusiast
(BACK! FORTH! BACK! FORTH! HARDER!!!)

The Excessive
Saliva Producer

MORE BATHROOM TEXTS WITH FRIENDS

he is telling me a story about "a friend" who used a straw to blow cocaine up a woman's butt last weekend.

not a friend.

not a friend.

watch yo straws.

THINGS THAT ARE DEFINITELY GOOD INFORMATION TO HAVE, BUT THAT DO NOT NEED TO BE SAID ON THE FIRST DATE:

"MY WIFE AND I TECHNICALLY STILL LIVE TOGETHER, BUT IT'S COOL: I SLEEP ON THE DAYBED USUALLY."

"I HAD CRABS ONCE. IT'S MOSTLY TREATED THOUGH."

"I REALLY WANT TO FUCK YOU RIGHT NOW."

"OH, I'M IN BETWEEN HOMES AT THE MOMENT. BUT I PARK AT MY BUDDY'S DRIVEWAY AND HE LETS ME SHOWER IN HIS PLACE, SO IT'S A PRETTY SWEET DEAL."

"I'M WORKING ON A NOVEL. IT'S ABOUT MY LIFE. I'LL SEND IT TO YOU."

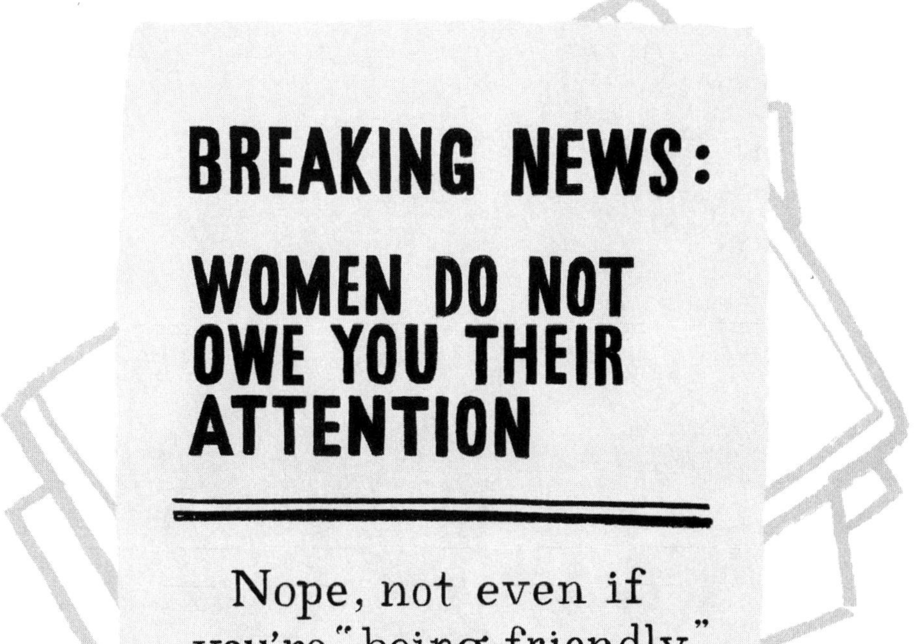
BREAKING NEWS:
WOMEN DO NOT OWE YOU THEIR ATTENTION
Nope, not even if you're "being friendly"

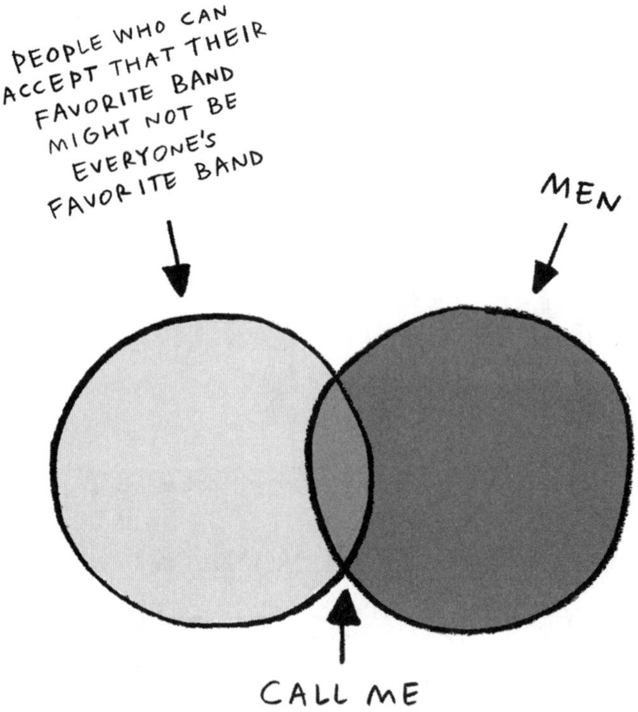
PEOPLE WHO CAN ACCEPT THAT THEIR FAVORITE BAND MIGHT NOT BE EVERYONE'S FAVORITE BAND
MEN
CALL ME

LEVEL of PHISH FANDOM

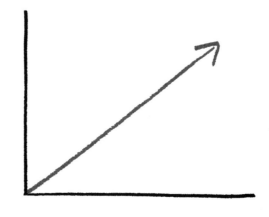

MALE PATTERN BALDNESS

UNTAPPED POTENTIAL

HOW TO BREAK UP WITH A PERSON
WITH WHOM YOU HAVE HAD A SERIOUS
RELATIONSHIP INVOLVING MUTUAL
DECLARATIONS OF LOVE AND CONCRETE
PLANS FOR THE FUTURE:

In Person

YES! ☑

LIKE THIS:

are we still getting dinner?

Today 5:22pm

is everything okay?

6:36pm

no

9:15 pm

What?

im sorry to leave you with that but cant talk until tmrw

...but...why are you not okay?!

i didn't want to do this over txt but ur making me

so

here it is

im going back to my ex

sorry

•••

TERRIBLE RELATIONSHIP ADVICE FROM

The Giving Tree:

IT'S TOTALLY COOL TO GO AHEAD AND TAKE
EVERYTHING YOU WANT FROM A WOMAN,
EVEN IF IT LEAVES HER LITERALLY AND/OR
METAPHORICALLY DESTROYED.

DON'T WORRY:

IF YOU'RE HAPPY, SHE'S HAPPY!

MARTYR

JERK

FIVE SHIRTS HE MOST DEFINITELY OWNS

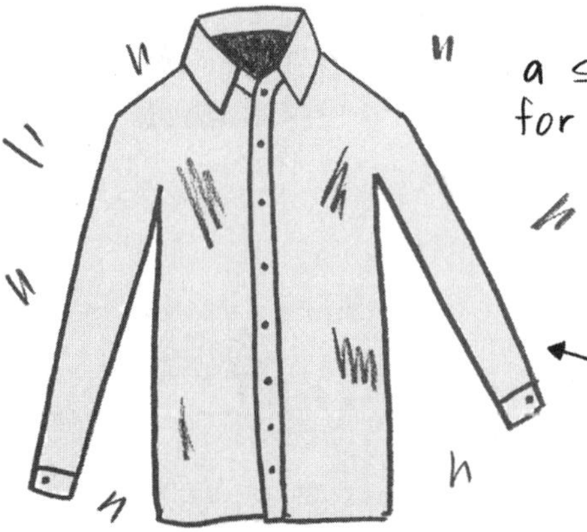

a shiny button-down for hitting the clurb

from Express circa 1997

an ironic t-shirt accidentally worn unironically

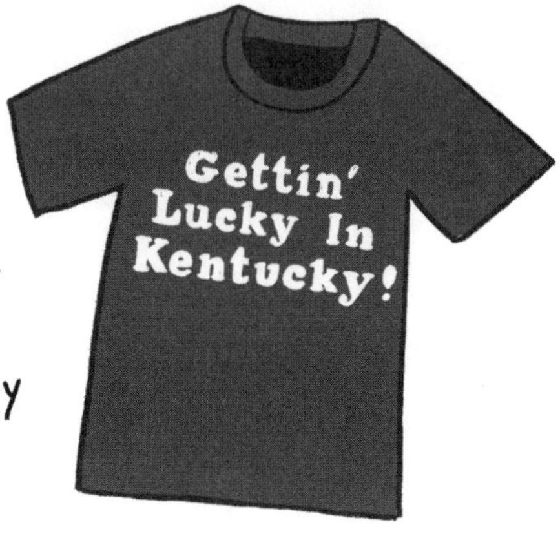
Gettin'
Lucky In
Kentucky!

A hi-larious shirt about beer.

HI-LARIOUS!

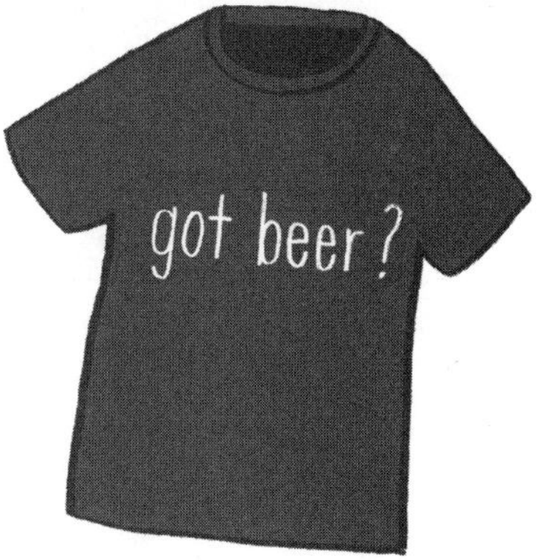
got beer?

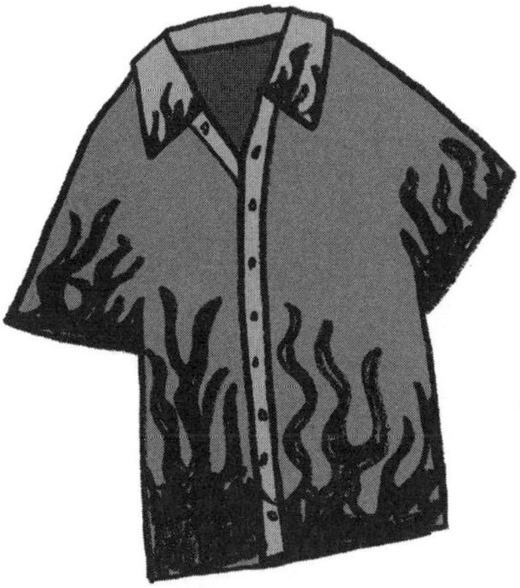

A shirt with flames on it.

Bonus points if the flames are WINGS.

A guayabera.

DENIRO WEARS THEM SOMETIMES, OK?

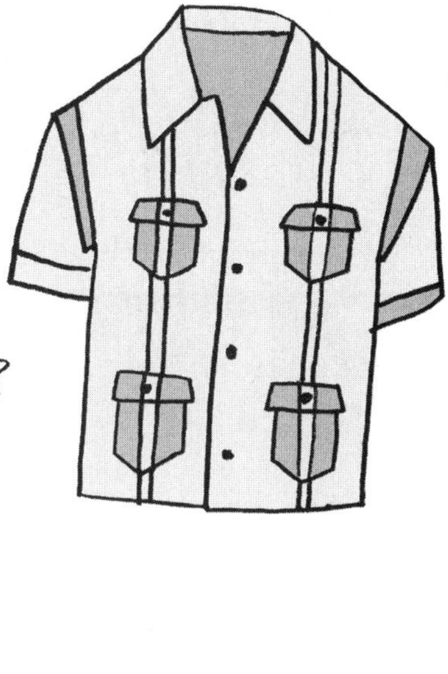

The More You Know™

IF A SHIRT SMELLS
BAD THE *first time*
IT IS *sniffed,*
IT WILL *continue*
TO SMELL BAD UPON
REPEATED *sniffs.*

GO-TO MEALS WHEN LEFT ALL ALONE

OLD
TACO
SHELLS

FRANKEN BERRY
CEREAL

MEAAAAAT

BLENDER

ANYTHING
THAT
BLENDS

"WORLD-FAMOUS"
"PERSONAL SPECIALTY"
* SOURCED FROM ALLRECIPES.COM

Things all boys do with their penises

- Hang a hand towel on it. SO BIG! SO STRONG!

- Measure it. Obviously.
  And frequently,
  just in case anything changed.

- Tuck it between their legs.
  Now they look like a GIRL!
  Hahahahahahaha.

- Bend it in half. Like a slinky!
  Except a penis!

- See if they can get it in their mouth.
  JUST TO CHECK.

FACT: PENISES SHOULD ONLY BE PRESENTED FOR VIEWING UPON DIRECT REQUEST.

These Sex Toys Actually Exist

(Sorry)

PLEATHER FLESHLIGHT HOLDER FOR THE CAR,
FOR THE STYLISH MASTURBATOR - ON - THE - GO

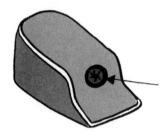

FLESHLIGHT GOES HERE
(WHEN DONE WITH COFFEE).

SQUISHY,
DISEMBODIED
FEET

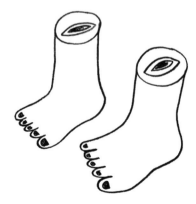

"LIPPY" SODA CAN

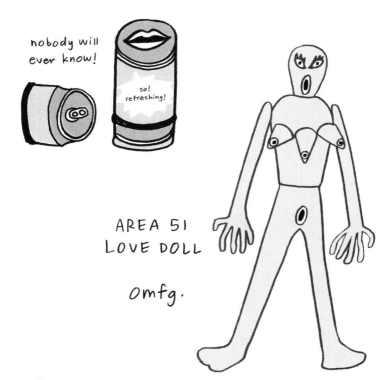

nobody will ever know!

so! refreshing!

AREA 51 LOVE DOLL

omfg.

hands off, kids!

BATHTUB DUCKIE MASSAGER

PRO-TIP:

If a man farts against the wall so it makes a louder sound, do not reward him by acknowledging what has just happened.

Much as with a small child, if you show any response at all, he will take that as a sign that he should do it again. And again. And again.

WTF-ERY THROUGHOUT HISTORY

THERE IS A TREE IN NIGER KNOWN AS "THE MOST ISOLATED TREE IN THE WORLD." IT IS SURROUNDED BY THE SAHARA DESERT, AND IS THE ONLY LANDMARK FOR 250 MILES. OR AT LEAST IT WAS UNTIL 1973, WHEN A TRUCK DRIVER MANAGED TO DRIVE INTO IT.

Actual Text Messages That Have Actually Been Sent by Actual Adult Humans:

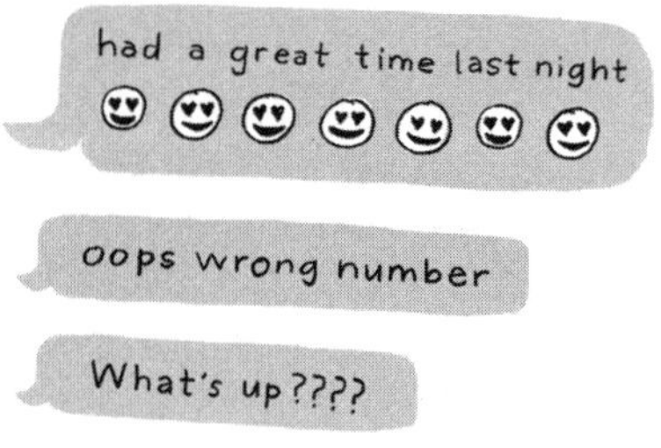
had a great time last night
oops wrong number
What's up????

In store. What aisle is the fruit in?

How long do you microwave popcorn for?

The baby is crying 😭 😬 ☹️ do you know why?

Babe what's my social security number?

I'm tired. Should I go to sleep?

Life's Great Truths

If a man secures one thing to another thing, he is physically compelled to shake said things, and then declare, loudly, to whomever is (or is not) present, "Well, THAT'S not going anywhere!"

A man will always try to towel off his balls before his face. By the next time he showers, he will feel secure in the knowledge that the towel will have forgotten which part went where, and be reset.

Telling a man "I almost fell and died getting out of my car" will never be understood as "Please shovel the driveway," just as "Goodness, it's getting late," will not be understood as "Please leave now."

Men can answer the question "What are you thinking about?" with "Nothing." And really, truly mean it. TRULY.

There is no greater satisfaction for a man than catching an item that has been tossed at him without warning.

WHATEVER
WOMEN DO,
THEY MUST DO
TWICE AS WELL
AS MEN TO
BE THOUGHT
HALF AS GOOD.
LUCKILY,
THIS IS NOT
DIFFICULT.

— Charlotte Whitton

ADD YOUR OWN
WTF-ery in the Wild :

Fine, Some of Them Are OK

As discussed in the disclaimer, there are, of course, exceptions to every rule.

There are also plenty of things about the males roaming among us that are actually quite lovely!

P.S. This is a short chapter.

MEN'S CHOICES TEND TO BE QUITE EASY TO UNPACK, SO LONG AS YOU REMEMBER THAT THEY ARE SIMPLE, SIMPLE CREATURES.

Did he not call?
He did not lose your number.
He did not die.
He just did not want to call you.

FUN FACT!

On average,
men have a higher resting body
temperature than women.

So in the winter, they basically
function as portable heaters.

Bonus if they snore:
white noise machine! sort of.

Men have great sweatshirts.
And pajama pants.
And sometimes forget to take their sweatshirts and pajama pants back after breakups!

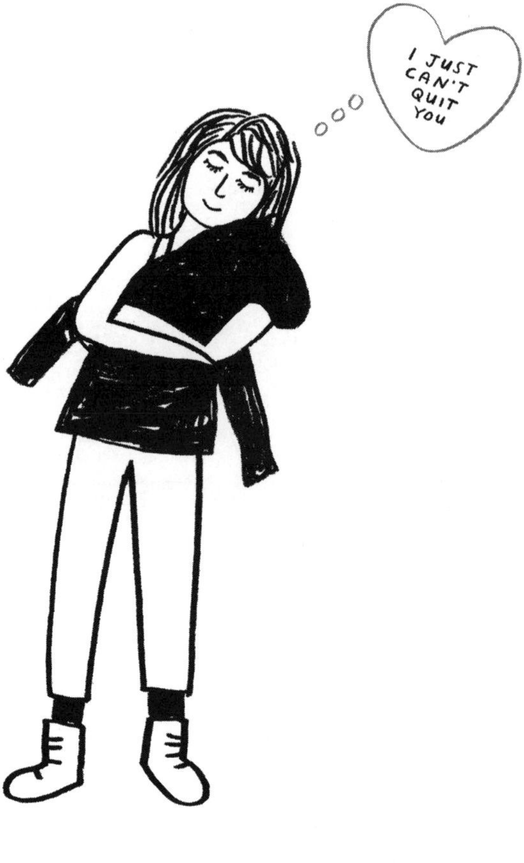
I JUST CAN'T QUIT YOU

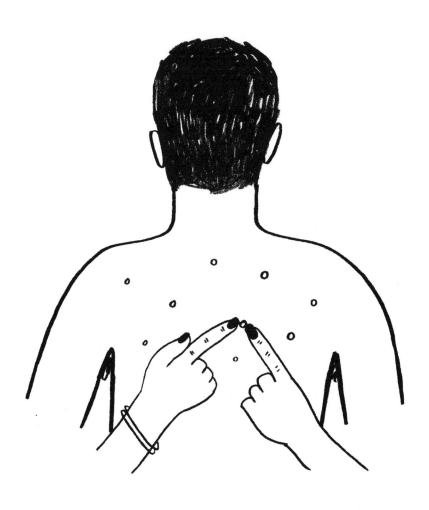

Men sometimes have backne. <u>FUN</u>.

If they are in a
bad mood,
you will know it,

Because they
will be awful.

Is He Mad ?

Does he seem mad ?

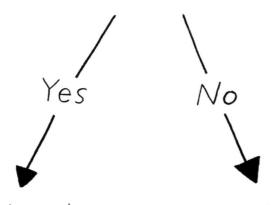

Yes

No

He is mad.

He is not mad.

And finally ...

Tom Hanks exists.

By all accounts, he's really nice.

Also see:

Hugh Jackman

LeBron James

Jon Stewart

George Clooney

Barack Obama

Stephen Colbert

Idris Elba

Mr. Rogers *

* technically deceased but it was already a short list.

⇒ EPILOGUE ⇐

HAVE ANY MEN IN YOUR LIFE RECENTLY
ACHIEVED ANY OF THE FOLLOWING?

- STOPPED HIMSELF FROM EXPLAINING A CONCEPT
  THAT HE A) DOESN'T UNDERSTAND HIMSELF
  AND B) IS INCAPABLE OF TALKING ABOUT
  WITHOUT SOUNDING CONDESCENDING?
  (SEE: MANSPLAINING.)

- AVOIDED SHOWING AND/OR MENTIONING HIS
  PENIS TO HIS COWORKERS (YES, ALL OF THEM)?

- EFFECTIVELY CARED FOR CHILDREN WITHOUT
  EXPECTING A PRIZE AT THE END?

- LET SOMEONE WITH A VAGINA EXPLAIN
  ANY ELEMENT OF FEMINISM?
  (WITHOUT INTERRUPTING? SEE AGAIN: MANSPLAINING.)

- EXPLAINED AN IDEA WITHOUT INCLUDING A SPORTS ANALOGY?

- DISPLAYED A SOLID UNDERSTANDING OF "PERSONAL SPACE"?

- ENTERTAINED THE POSSIBILITY THAT MAYBE - JUST MAYBE - SOMETHING WASN'T ABOUT HIM?

AMAZING.

MAKE SURE YOU TELL HIM HOW GREAT HE IS. LIKE, OVER AND OVER.

REMEMBER:

REINFORCEMENT IS KEY.

This book was inspired by conversations with virtually all of the women in my life. But really, the story that made me actually write the thing was "The Tale of the Old Waters." So Erin (and, by proxy, Cameron): Thank you. You made a book called Seriously WTF is Wrong with Men happen, and I think the world is better for it.

Biggest thanks go to our kick-ass editor, Nina Shield, who has spent years supporting all my weird little ideas.

The team at TarcherPerigee is an eternal joy to work with— Allyssa Fortunato, Sara Johnson, Carla Iannone, Marian Lizzi, Megan Newman, Hannah Steigmeyer, Claire Winecoff, Nancy Resnick, thank you. Kim Perel, you agent like no other. And finally, big love to my witches. You know who you are.

JORDAN REID lives in Malibu with various kids and pets. She is the coauthor of the Big Activity Book series and the founding editor of RamshackleGlam.com, where she writes daily about things she probably shouldn't. She is, perhaps unsurprisingly, divorced.

KELLY LASSERRE is a freelance illustrator and hand-letterer. Since receiving a BFA in illustration, she has been creating drawings and paintings for various books, magazines, design studios, and commissioned art projects. Kelly lives in Philadelphia, where she works hard to keep her houseplants and herself alive and well.